© CARDIEN DESIGN CO.

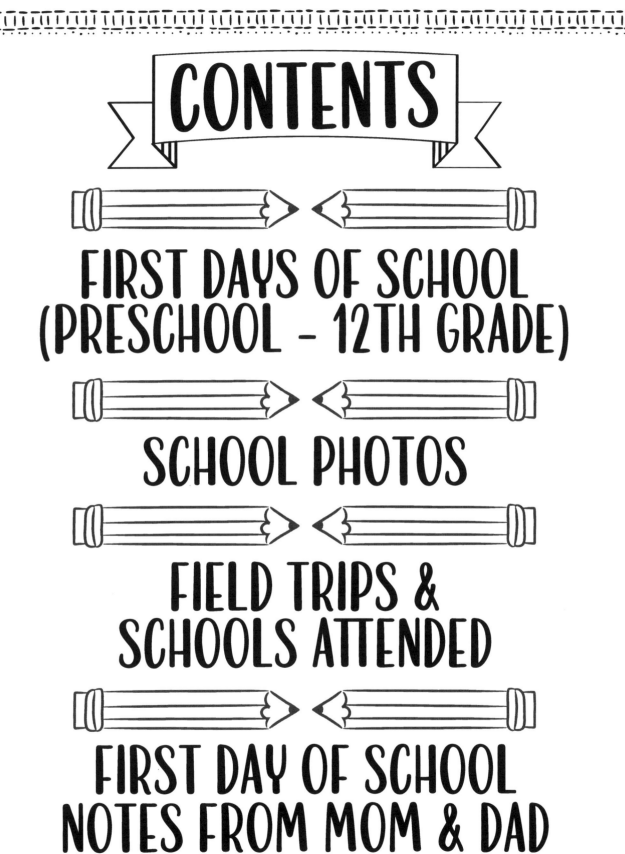

THE FIRST DAY OF EACH GRADE

ON MY 1ST DAY OF PRESCHOOL

DATE OF 1ST DAY

AGE: _____ HEIGHT: _____

OUTFIT: _____

NAME OF SCHOOL: _____

NAME OF TEACHER: _____

CURRENT FAVORITES

TV SHOW: _____ MOVIE: _____

BOOK: _____ SONG: _____

THING TO DO: _____

PLACE TO GO: _____

PART OF SCHOOL: _____

GROUPS OR ACTIVITIES: _____

BEST FRIEND: _____

PETS: _____

ANY BIG CHANGES SINCE LAST YEAR: _____

WHEN I GROW UP I WANT TO BE A: _____

ON MY 1ST DAY OF PRESCHOOL

A PLACE FOR PHOTOS, DRAWINGS, OR THOUGHTS

MY SIGNATURE:

ON MY 1ST DAY OF KINDERGARTEN

DATE OF 1ST DAY

AGE: _____ HEIGHT: _____

OUTFIT: _____

NAME OF SCHOOL: _____

NAME OF TEACHER: _____

CURRENT FAVORITES

TV SHOW: _____

MOVIE: _____

BOOK: _____

SONG: _____

THING TO DO: _____

PLACE TO GO: _____

PART OF SCHOOL: _____

GROUPS OR ACTIVITIES: _____

BEST FRIEND: _____

PETS: _____

ANY BIG CHANGES SINCE LAST YEAR: _____

WHEN I GROW UP I WANT TO BE A: _____

ON MY 1ST DAY OF KINDERGARTEN

A PLACE FOR PHOTOS, DRAWINGS, OR THOUGHTS

MY SIGNATURE:

ON MY 1ST DAY OF 1ST GRADE

DATE OF 1ST DAY

AGE: _____ HEIGHT: _____

OUTFIT: _____

NAME OF SCHOOL: _____

NAME OF TEACHER: _____

CURRENT FAVORITES

TV SHOW: _____ MOVIE: _____

BOOK: _____ SONG: _____

THING TO DO: _____

PLACE TO GO: _____

PART OF SCHOOL: _____

GROUPS OR ACTIVITIES: _____

BEST FRIEND: _____

PETS: _____

ANY BIG CHANGES SINCE LAST YEAR: _____

WHEN I GROW UP I WANT TO BE A: _____
_____

ON MY 1ST DAY OF 1ST GRADE

A PLACE FOR PHOTOS, DRAWINGS, OR THOUGHTS

MY SIGNATURE:

ON MY 1ST DAY OF 2ND GRADE

DATE OF 1ST DAY

AGE: _____ HEIGHT: _____

OUTFIT: _____

NAME OF SCHOOL: _____

NAME OF TEACHER: _____

CURRENT FAVORITES

TV SHOW: _____ MOVIE: _____

BOOK: _____ SONG: _____

THING TO DO: _____

PLACE TO GO: _____

PART OF SCHOOL: _____

GROUPS OR ACTIVITIES: _____

BEST FRIEND: _____

PETS: _____

ANY BIG CHANGES SINCE LAST YEAR: _____

WHEN I GROW UP I WANT TO BE A: _____

_____

ON MY 1ST DAY OF 2ND GRADE

A PLACE FOR PHOTOS, DRAWINGS, OR THOUGHTS

MY SIGNATURE:

ON MY 1ST DAY OF 3RD GRADE

DATE OF 1ST DAY

AGE: _____ HEIGHT: _____

OUTFIT: _____

NAME OF SCHOOL: _____

NAME OF TEACHER: _____

CURRENT FAVORITES

TV SHOW: _____   MOVIE: _____

BOOK: _____   SONG: _____

THING TO DO: _____

PLACE TO GO: _____

PART OF SCHOOL: _____

GROUPS OR ACTIVITIES: _____

BEST FRIEND: _____

PETS: _____

ANY BIG CHANGES SINCE LAST YEAR: _____

WHEN I GROW UP I WANT TO BE A: _____

ON MY 1ST DAY OF 3RD GRADE

A PLACE FOR PHOTOS, DRAWINGS, OR THOUGHTS

MY SIGNATURE:

ON MY 1ST DAY OF 4TH GRADE

DATE OF 1ST DAY

AGE: _____ HEIGHT: _____

OUTFIT: _____

NAME OF SCHOOL: _____

NAME OF TEACHER: _____

CURRENT FAVORITES

TV SHOW: _____ MOVIE: _____

BOOK: _____ SONG: _____

THING TO DO: _____

PLACE TO GO: _____

PART OF SCHOOL: _____

GROUPS OR ACTIVITIES: _____

BEST FRIEND: _____

PETS: _____

ANY BIG CHANGES SINCE LAST YEAR: _____

WHEN I GROW UP I WANT TO BE A: _____

ON MY 1ST DAY OF 4TH GRADE

A PLACE FOR PHOTOS, DRAWINGS, OR THOUGHTS

MY SIGNATURE: _____

ON MY 1ST DAY OF 5TH GRADE

DATE OF 1ST DAY

AGE: _____ HEIGHT: _____

OUTFIT: _____

NAME OF SCHOOL: _____

NAME OF TEACHER: _____

CURRENT FAVORITES

TV SHOW: _____ MOVIE: _____

BOOK: _____ SONG: _____

THING TO DO: _____

PLACE TO GO: _____

PART OF SCHOOL: _____

GROUPS OR ACTIVITIES: _____

BEST FRIEND: _____

PETS: _____

ANY BIG CHANGES SINCE LAST YEAR: _____

WHEN I GROW UP I WANT TO BE A: _____

ON MY 1ST DAY OF 5TH GRADE

A PLACE FOR PHOTOS, DRAWINGS, OR THOUGHTS

MY SIGNATURE:

ON MY 1ST DAY OF 6TH GRADE

DATE OF 1ST DAY

AGE: _____ HEIGHT: _____
OUTFIT: _____
NAME OF SCHOOL: _____
NAME OF TEACHER: _____

CURRENT FAVORITES

TV SHOW: _____ MOVIE: _____
BOOK: _____ SONG: _____
THING TO DO: _____
PLACE TO GO: _____
PART OF SCHOOL: _____

GROUPS OR ACTIVITIES: _____
BEST FRIEND: _____
PETS: _____
ANY BIG CHANGES SINCE LAST YEAR: _____
WHEN I GROW UP I WANT TO BE A: _____

ON MY 1ST DAY OF 6TH GRADE

A PLACE FOR PHOTOS, DRAWINGS, OR THOUGHTS

MY SIGNATURE:

ON MY 1ST DAY OF 7TH GRADE

DATE OF 1ST DAY

AGE: _____ HEIGHT: _____

OUTFIT: _____

NAME OF SCHOOL: _____

NAME OF TEACHER: _____

CURRENT FAVORITES

TV SHOW: _____ MOVIE: _____

BOOK: _____ SONG: _____

THING TO DO: _____

PLACE TO GO: _____

PART OF SCHOOL: _____

GROUPS OR ACTIVITIES: _____

BEST FRIEND: _____

PETS: _____

ANY BIG CHANGES SINCE LAST YEAR: _____

WHEN I GROW UP I WANT TO BE A: _____

_____

ON MY 1ST DAY OF 7TH GRADE

A PLACE FOR PHOTOS, DRAWINGS, OR THOUGHTS

MY SIGNATURE:

ON MY 1ST DAY OF 8TH GRADE

DATE OF 1ST DAY

AGE: _____ HEIGHT: _____

OUTFIT: _____

NAME OF SCHOOL: _____

NAME OF TEACHER: _____

CURRENT FAVORITES

TV SHOW: _____   MOVIE: _____

BOOK: _____   SONG: _____

THING TO DO: _____

PLACE TO GO: _____

PART OF SCHOOL: _____

GROUPS OR ACTIVITIES: _____

BEST FRIEND: _____

PETS: _____

ANY BIG CHANGES SINCE LAST YEAR: _____

WHEN I GROW UP I WANT TO BE A: _____

ON MY 1ST DAY OF 8TH GRADE

A PLACE FOR PHOTOS, DRAWINGS, OR THOUGHTS

MY SIGNATURE:

ON MY 1ST DAY OF 9TH GRADE

DATE OF 1ST DAY

AGE: _____ HEIGHT: _____

OUTFIT: _____

NAME OF SCHOOL: _____

NAME OF TEACHER: _____

CURRENT FAVORITES

TV SHOW: _____ MOVIE: _____

BOOK: _____ SONG: _____

THING TO DO: _____

PLACE TO GO: _____

PART OF SCHOOL: _____

GROUPS OR ACTIVITIES: _____

BEST FRIEND: _____

PETS: _____

ANY BIG CHANGES SINCE LAST YEAR: _____

WHEN I GROW UP I WANT TO BE A: _____
_____

ON MY 1ST DAY OF 9TH GRADE

A PLACE FOR PHOTOS, DRAWINGS, OR THOUGHTS

MY SIGNATURE:

ON MY 1ST DAY OF 10TH GRADE

DATE OF 1ST DAY

AGE: _____ HEIGHT: _____

OUTFIT: _____

NAME OF SCHOOL: _____

NAME OF TEACHER: _____

CURRENT FAVORITES

TV SHOW: _____ MOVIE: _____

BOOK: _____ SONG: _____

THING TO DO: _____

PLACE TO GO: _____

PART OF SCHOOL: _____

GROUPS OR ACTIVITIES: _____

BEST FRIEND: _____

PETS: _____

ANY BIG CHANGES SINCE LAST YEAR: _____

WHEN I GROW UP I WANT TO BE A: _____

ON MY 1ST DAY OF 10TH GRADE

A PLACE FOR PHOTOS, DRAWINGS, OR THOUGHTS

MY SIGNATURE:

ON MY 1ST DAY OF 11TH GRADE

DATE OF 1ST DAY

AGE: _____ HEIGHT: _____

OUTFIT: _____

NAME OF SCHOOL: _____

NAME OF TEACHER: _____

CURRENT FAVORITES

TV SHOW: _____ MOVIE: _____

BOOK: _____ SONG: _____

THING TO DO: _____

PLACE TO GO: _____

PART OF SCHOOL: _____

GROUPS OR ACTIVITIES: _____

BEST FRIEND: _____

PETS: _____

ANY BIG CHANGES SINCE LAST YEAR: _____

WHEN I GROW UP I WANT TO BE A: _____
_____

ON MY 1ST DAY OF 11TH GRADE

A PLACE FOR PHOTOS, DRAWINGS, OR THOUGHTS

MY SIGNATURE:

ON MY 1ST DAY OF 12TH GRADE

DATE OF 1ST DAY

AGE: _____ HEIGHT: _____

OUTFIT: _____

NAME OF SCHOOL: _____

NAME OF TEACHER: _____

CURRENT FAVORITES

TV SHOW: _____

BOOK: _____

MOVIE: _____

SONG: _____

THING TO DO: _____

PLACE TO GO: _____

PART OF SCHOOL: _____

GROUPS OR ACTIVITIES: _____

BEST FRIEND: _____

PETS: _____

ANY BIG CHANGES SINCE LAST YEAR: _____

WHEN I GROW UP I WANT TO BE A: _____

ON MY 1ST DAY OF 12TH GRADE

A PLACE FOR PHOTOS, DRAWINGS, OR THOUGHTS

MY SIGNATURE:

SCHOOL PHOTOS

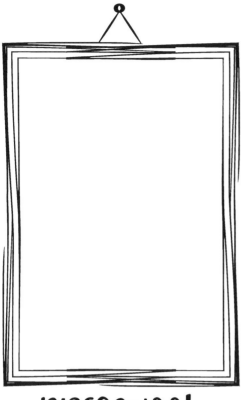

PRESCHOOL

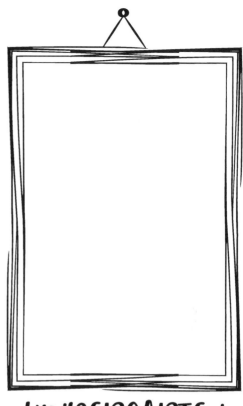

KINDERGARTEN

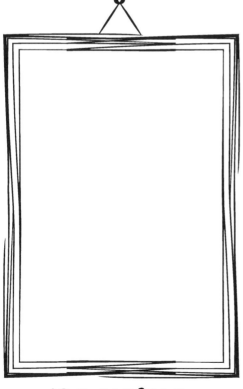

1ST GRADE

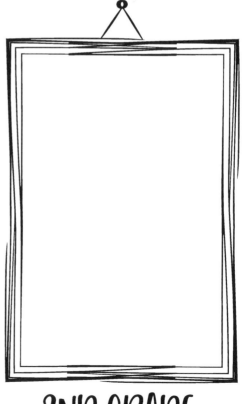

2ND GRADE

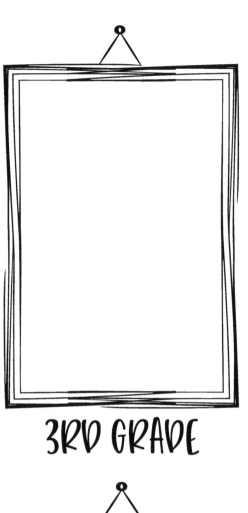
3RD GRADE

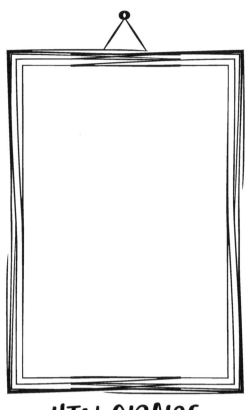
4TH GRADE

5TH GRADE

6TH GRADE

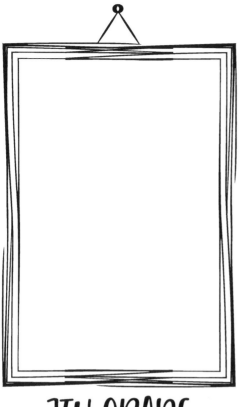
7TH GRADE

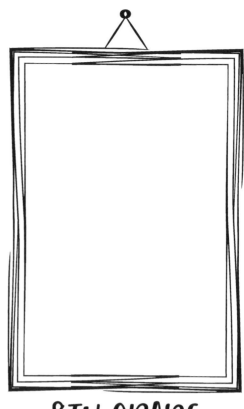
8TH GRADE

9TH GRADE

10TH GRADE

FIELD TRIPS AND SCHOOLS ATTENDED

FIELD TRIPS

WHERE TO	GRADE	DATE OF TRIP

FIELD TRIPS

WHERE TO	GRADE	DATE OF TRIP

FIELD TRIPS

WHERE TO	GRADE	DATE OF TRIP

SCHOOLS ATTENDED

SCHOOL NAME & LOCATION	GRADES ATTENDED

NOTES FROM MOM & DAD

First Day Notes from Mom & Dad

Write a quick line or two to your son or daughter at the start of each school year. When they graduate they'll be able to look back on all your notes to them as they grew up through the years!

PRESCHOOL:

KINDERGARTEN:

1ST GRADE:

2ND GRADE:

3RD GRADE:

4TH GRADE:

5TH GRADE:

6TH GRADE:

7TH GRADE:

8TH GRADE:

9TH GRADE:

10TH GRADE:

11TH GRADE:

12TH GRADE:

AT YOUR GRADUATION,

Love, _____

HAPPY GRADUATION!

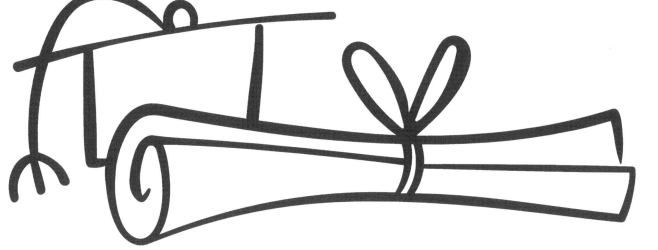

Made in the USA
Coppell, TX
09 August 2023